THIS APRIL DAY

DISCARD

WEST GA REG LIB SYS
Neva Lomason
Memorial Library

OTHER BOOKS
BY JUDSON MITCHAM

FICTION
The Sweet Everlasting

POETRY
Somewhere in Ecclesiastes
Notes for a Prayer in June

THIS APRIL DAY

JUDSON MITCHAM

Poems

Anhinga Press, 2003
Tallahassee, Florida

Copyright © Judson Mitcham 2003

All rights reserved under
International and Pan-American Copyright Conventions.

*No portion of this book may be reproduced in any form without
the written permission of the publisher, except by a reviewer,
who may quote brief passages in connection with a review
for a magazine or newspaper.*

Cover design, book design and production – C.L. Knight
Author photo – Art Butler
Cover photo – C.L. Knight
Typesetting – titles in Trajan; text in Esprit

Library of Congress Cataloging-in-Publication Data
This April Day by Judson Mitcham – First Edition
ISBN 0938078-73-9
Library of Congress Card Number: 2002115287

*This publication is sponsored in part by a grant
from the Florida Department of State,
Division of Cultural Affairs,
and the Florida Arts Council.*

Anhinga Press Inc. is a nonprofit corporation
dedicated wholly to the publication
and appreciation of fine poetry.

For personal orders, catalogs
and information write to:
Anhinga Press
P.O. Box 10595
Tallahassee, FL 32302
Web site: www.anhinga.org
E-mail: info@anhinga.org

Published in the United States
by Anhinga Press
Tallahassee, Florida
First Edition, 2003

For Myrtle and Wilson

CONTENTS

ix   Acknowledgments

3   History of Rain

4   Dream Laughter

5   Preface to an Omnibus Review

7   The Mystery

8   Philosophy, With Illustrations

9   Comedian

11   Two Poems for My Father

13   Peace on Earth

14   Halloween at the Nursing Home

15   Writing

16   In Memory of Adrienne Bond

17   Homage

19   Boys Playing Ball After Dark

20   The Funerals of Strangers

21   Together

22   The Drifting Blue

23   Click

25   Homework

26   The Secret

27   Some Words for Bill Matthews

28   The Question

34   Two Love Letters

36   The Foolishness of God is Wiser than Men

37   Elegy for a Young Poet

38   A World Beneath

43   Prayer

44   Calvin's Wife

46   Going Home

47   Laughter

51   The Widow's Desire

56   The Multitude

58   Sustenance

59   Home

60   Surrender

61   Desire

63   A Postcard to My Father

64   In the Sweet By and By

67   An Introduction

71   About the author

ACKNOWLEDGMENTS

Poems in this collection, or versions of them, first appeared in the following:

America — "Philosophy, with Illustrations"

Chattahoochee Review — "Boys Playing Ball after Dark"

Denver Quarterly — "Two Love Letters"

Georgia Journal — "Homework"

Georgia Review — "An Introduction," "Going Home," "Preface to an Omnibus Review," "Surrender," "Prayer," "History of Rain"

Gettysburg Review — "In the Sweet By and By," "Together"

Habersham Review — "Peace on Earth," "The Question," "Desire," "Halloween at the Nursing Home," "Sustenance"

New England Review — "Dream Laughter," "The Secret," "A Postcard to My Father," "Writing," "Homage"

Poetry — "The Foolishness of God is Wiser Than Men"

River Styx — "Click," "The Widow's Desire"

Snake Nation Review — "In Memory of Adrienne Bond"

Southern Review — "Comedian," "The Mystery," "A World Beneath"

"Preface to an Omnibus Review" was reprinted in *Harper's*.

THIS APRIL DAY

HISTORY OF RAIN

What if every prayer for rain brought it down?
What if prayer made drunks quit the bars, numbers hit,
the right girl smile, shirts tumble from the dryer
fully ironed? What if God

required no more than a word? Every spot
of cancer would dissolve like peppermint,
every heart pump blood through arteries as clean
as drinking straws then. All grief would be gone,

all reverence and wonder. But if rain
should fall only once in a thousand years, rare
as a comet, if for fifty generations
there was never that sweet hint of metal in the air

until late one April afternoon
when the dust began to swirl above the ballfield,
and the first big drops fell, popping in the dirt,
and sudden as a thought, great gray-white sheets

steamed on the asphalt, fought with the pines,
would we all not walk out trying to believe
our place in the history of rain? We'd be there
for the shining of the world:

the weeds made gaudy with the quicksilver breeze;
the rainbows floating over black-glass streets;
each cupped thing bright with its blessing; and long
afterwards, a noise like praise, the rain

still falling in the trees.

DREAM LAUGHTER

I conveyed an odd rumor to my brother:
our father was alive in his grave. So we dug,
struck the box, hauled him out, and they were right.

Just in case, we had brought the kitchen table
and a Sunday meal — beef, rolls and gravy,
our mother's chocolate cake. He turned away,

raised a hand to his long ragged beard.
I asked him how he was. Eyes flat,
he answered me with one word, *Dead*,
his timing still deft, nothing lost from the voice
often comic with the obvious in life,
and the three of us laughed like fools. I awoke

with his bony hands grabbing for the rolls.

PREFACE TO AN OMNIBUS REVIEW

Do not write poems about poetry. Commit
no epigraphs, object poems, homages to anyone.
Please, no more elegies for your father. No details
of your grandmother's hands. Leave the sepia
photographs alone.
                    Give us no
Guggenheim-and-here-I-am, bored-or-overwhelmed
poetry. Don't write about divorce — no ironic
meditations at the playground or the game.
Nothing on the limits of the language.
                                        Construct
no ugly poems ragged on the page, but nothing square.
Go easy on the birds and the trees. No asleep-
in-the-deer-stand, waking-to-an-eight-point-buck-
only-thirty-yards-away kind of poetry.
                                        And no
remember-that-cafe-in-San Diego poems
of heartbreak; not one Rilke imitation;
nothing modeled on the Spanish; nothing spoken
as Osip Mandelstam or Akhmatova.
                                    If ever,
on a clear summer night,
there's a baseball diamond in a small town, a field
lighted like a scene in a glass paperweight,
an old man loud in the stands — don't even think it.

If there's something you believe in, have the decency
to keep it to yourself — no revelations, no irate
manifestos on the Earth or deconstructions of the bed,

no upper case god. There should be no nuns,
no old Baptist hymns in your poetry.

        Employ
everything you need to make it happen,
that momentary stay against confusion, but include
no catalogs, no dogs.

THE MYSTERY

"… how great is the mystery that looks out
of the eyes of a dog …"
— Margaret Washburn, *The Animal Mind,* 1912

Grown as old in her own years now
as anyone in town, Cleopatra,
deaf and blind, lies quietly all day

on the cool front stoop, flaps her tail
smelling roast beef lowered to her bowl —
a lean, tender cut. The only sinners

in the universe, the only true dreamers
of eternity or even
another day, the only great explainers

can't explain, absolutely,
why a man might cry for his dog
harder than he did for his father;

though the man nearly knows
as he opens that hole in the back yard,
works to make it deep, breathing in

the sweetness of the earth.

PHILOSOPHY, WITH ILLUSTRATIONS

The paperback history of thought
cost fifteen cents. I discovered it
in a box of old books at a junk store, where
it now belonged, ruined by a child

with crayons, who had reddened Heraclitus, and who,
as if choosing to ignore or revere
every word set down in between,
had brightened up Schopenhauer, bearing down hard

with an orange and a green. Standing there
waiting on the book's once blank last page
is a figure with its arms set to fly;
with a body like a one-lane road;

with fingers like the petals of a sunflower, head
ballooned, hair floating just above
like a cloudy idea or a cloud;
with hollow round eyes drawn large; with perhaps

a smile, though it's easily a grimace,
on its one thick deep blue lip.

COMEDIAN

When I sang those lines about Christ, who arose,
so the author of the hymn would have had it,
with a "triumph o'er his foes," I was four years old,
and proclaimed he had triumphed "o'er his clothes."

This provokes no more than a smile now,
as everything resides in the timing and the voice,
the occasion of surprise, but when my parents,
sitting at the kitchen table, heard my mistake,
they twisted and they bent like pines in the wind;
they howled and they coughed, until they both
crossed over into grief,
then grabbed me up and hugged me while I struggled,
angry and confused.
                          One afternoon,
working in the basement — I can't remember why,
but everyone was down there watching — my father
hit his head on a pipe, and the dull hollow bonk
of his skull meeting steel,
and then that expression on his face — less of pain
than of disbelief — set us all off,
nearly dropped my mother to the floor. I recall
them sitting on the steps in the half-dark,
how she laid his head over on her shoulder.

In the last two years of his life, my father
discovered that he couldn't pray aloud. His voice
thickened and it broke,
so that finally he asked to be excused
if the preacher called his name, and so he failed
to negotiate grace when we gathered
with our families.

I think about the day
I saw him at the newly closed grave of his brother —
the only one younger, whose protector he had been
as a child — now dead by his own hand.
He might have been mistaken from a distance
for a man overtaken by a joke,
from the rhythm of his shoulders. When he laughed,

my father nearly barked his delight, gave a sharp
exhalation of surprise.
                        I heard it happen
on the telephone the last time we talked. And if I
could sing with a child's wrong praise, even now,
I'd become that comedian of innocence again
gladly — to be gathered in their arms, baffled
by the sorrow that is not what it seems;
to be hurt once more by the laughter.

TWO POEMS FOR MY FATHER

I. The Prize

He still gets mail. Eight years in the grave,
he's achieved a kind of postal immortality.
A store keeps sending him its catalog; it wants
to know if he is ready for the winter. He receives
cruise information — you deserve to get away,
the letter will suggest. Unaware
how accurate they are, others write
telling him in large block letters
he's been chosen as a finalist. Yes,
he's now among the few who have qualified. In fact,
he may have won already, they will say, and he has,
he has. And how he gloried in the prize
they're offering: the chance of a lifetime.

II. April 9

Today, my father's ten years old in heaven,
and he doesn't yet know what it is, this place
where the plate is a washed-out spot in the dirt,
first is a feed sack, second base and third,
wood scraps. Here,
there's a chickenwire fence, then a dirt road.
And on the other side of that, in the afternoons,
the women like to sit, shelling butterbeans.
The sky here still turns red beyond the pines,
and when the breeze brings a single smell —
call it what you will —
of blossom, weeds, the broken earth, the rain;
when the crickets in the tall grass quit, all at once,
so the afternoon stalls where it is;
when his mother's shout rises from the house,
like nothing in a dream, and calls him home,
he is so filled then
with old, sad delight that day is done,
he knows, but then forgets, where he has gone.

PEACE ON EARTH

— Women's Correctional Institute, Hardwick, Ga.

The house close by goes dark after Christmas,
but the prison keeps lit year round; looped wire
shines like tinsel in a nightmare.

Inside, when they've written what I asked for,
some memory that's vivid with detail,
I am not quite ready.
                    If I think about Eve,
think of evil introduced into the world,
I remember how the snake liked to talk,
and I talk a little more.
                    Every night,
when I leave this place, I'm a free man, held
by the histories of women.
                    When the roads
open as they've never done before,
the women tell their stories in my head:
so many jagged scars for loving men;
                            God,
so many still pinned between Daddy and the bed.

Uneasy in my body, I have heard
a sentence fall apart, a woman's voice
choking on the thanks for what is hers,

for peace at last, for locks on all the doors.

HALLOWEEN AT THE NURSING HOME

Every year, first day of October, there they are:
the sudden undead in the hallways;
the cartoon tombstones; too many skeletons
                              ready to dance;
and all those crones on brooms whose eyes gleam
and threaten, as though
they had flown in only to discover
they can never leave.
                    In time,
Thanksgiving will come,

but all October, the little ghosts,
one for each blade of the dining hall fans,
spin above the tables. They whirl, they celebrate
like handpuppets set free of the body,

their skirts flaring out on the long
                              carnival ride of the afterlife.
As if giddy with forever, they sweep
above the uncovered heads of the old women,
who do not look up.

WRITING

But prayer was not enough, after all, for my father.
His last two brothers died five weeks apart.
He couldn't get to sleep, had no appetite, sat
staring. Though he prayed,
he could find no peace until he tried
to write about his brothers, tell a story
for each one: Perry's long travail
with the steamfitters' union, which he worked for;
and Harvey — here the handwriting changes,
he bears down — Harvey loved his children.

I discovered those few sheets of paper
as I looked through my father's old Bible
on the morning of his funeral. The others
in the family had seen them long ago;
they had all known the story,
and they told me I had not, most probably, because
I am a writer,
and my father was embarrassed by his effort. Yet
who has seen him as I can: risen

in the middle of the night, bending over
the paper, working close
to the heart of all greatness, he is so lost.

IN MEMORY OF ADRIENNE BOND

A great poem does not end. It will go on
inside the lucky ones who've heard it well,
who've caught its praise. And Adrienne was one.

A poem lays down the haze of winter dawn
to make us know some story we must tell
until we tell it right. It still goes on,

that spell against the night, that quiet song
made well, to hold the sad, the beautiful.
Few sing like that, but Adrienne was one.

There is no music deep enough to mourn
this woman whom we loved, no words to fill
our empty page but hers. And they go on

and say our names and tell us what we've known:
she moved within our lives as no one will.
This April day when Adrienne is gone,

oh there is something broken in us all,
and that same thing is singing in us still.
A great poem does not end. It will go on.
It does go on. And Adrienne is one.

HOMAGE

"Let us now praise famous men, and our fathers ..."
— Ecclesiasticus 44:1

Our family in the 1930s was not
far different, if at all, from the Ricketts or the Gudgers.
In the old photographs, I have seen
the same angry squint, as if a boy
were shaken, unbelieving, from oblivion,
only minutes after coming from the cottonfield —
his backbone throbbing like a bad tooth —
to return, hauling buckets of molasses
with arsenic to spread against the army worms,
the egg-laying flies and the boll weevil.
                                        Still,
it is not that connection I would make.
I think of James Agee and his gift. Even though,
in the sawmarked grain
of the sharecroppers' bare pine walls, he discovered —
swirling in the reds and peasant golds —
a poetry of agate and of silk, in the end,
he'd have chosen no words,
would have lifted up slivers of wood, bits of cloth,
musty lumps of earth to tell the story.
                                    And for me,
since a morning last April,
Agee puts it well: "a piece of body torn out
by the roots" would be truer than my words. But tonight,
only with my words,
I am holding up a King James Bible, inscribed
in 1942 by my mother,
and carried through the war, then forty more years,
the waxy black pebble-grain skin rubbed gray,

with patches like chamois to the hands, every page
ragged and frayed, and the gospels freed
from the spine.
               I am raising this Bible,
which is lying at his right hand, still, to let it praise
anyone, famous man or humble, whom it will.

BOYS PLAYING BALL AFTER DARK

— in memory of Raymond Andrews

A man takes a walk one afternoon
when the red sun's guttering in the pines,

and he doesn't wear a coat, though it's cold.
There's no one on the road. He will recall

the sweetness in the air, the burning leaves,
but this is what he loves:

discovering the boys playing ball
out of season, for as long as it is possible,

and the game going on after that,
so the boy at bat sees the silhouette

of the other child moving on the sky,
but not the ball, thrown and on its way.

He doesn't stop and interrupt their game
but still can hear their voices back at home,

and so he gives them names, he lets them talk,
he offers them a world, as from the dark,

he returns once again to his work.

THE FUNERALS OF STRANGERS

The funerals of strangers make us late,
delay us on the road, slow us down.

When the cars ease by, lights on, we will wait
patiently at first, but if the whole town

turns out, showing how it mourns, we can get
vexed at the dead, whose passing overflowed

the church close by, whose burial will set
a record for its holding of the road.

We do see clearly who we are, sitting there:
we're not the one followed to the graveyard.

And so, though we raise our arms in despair,
grimace, grip the steering wheel hard,

a quick thrill flickers in us all, looking on,
as it did inside that stranger, who is gone.

TOGETHER

When my father died,
I wanted everything to stop as he passed by,
the faces of the whole world turning like a field
of sunflowers then.

And when a car backfires on the highway now,
every starling in the graveyard hovers near the earth,
then the flock swerves off like a black veil
swirling in the wind.

We stood there looking at the grave,
and my tears didn't come, this time,
until I turned to my mother,
and I saw hers.

We are sitting on a cold stone bench,
and when the flock startles upward with the noise,
my mother's hand tightens on mine, and she says
"Goodness," nothing else.

Goodness indeed, I am thinking. The birds
turn together in the air above the dead.

THE DRIFTING BLUE

At the table near mine in the airport bar
they're whispering in a tongue I cannot name,
and still, I have to listen. Maybe she

is asking, *Will you miss me?* He could say,
for all I'll ever know, *You are the dream
that filled me as a child, that meant the world*

would open like a blossom. Then their time
is nearly gone, they've almost said goodbye,
their whispers turning rough. *And I will bring*

the drifting blue itself, I hear her promising,
I hear it when she's gone, *and I will bring
the light along the edge of everything.*

CLICK

"… a poem comes right with a click, like a box."
— William Butler Yeats

There's the box-and-one, too:
a two-two zone with the free man badgering the hotshot,
denying him the ball. Every day,

the shooter's in the gym,
where he makes these demands of himself: half an hour
of full-court sprints, alternating with foul shots;

fifty ten-footers off the board, right and left,
off the dribble; fifty jumpers from the top of the key,
fifty each from the corners and the wings. Most often,

he's alone, and he takes it all in:
how a single dark board splits the lane,
how the empty gym booms with the ball, how it echoes

with the squeaking of his shoes. This is not
optional, the pause just to gaze across the court
when the hardwood shines like the calm, deep heart

of McElroy's Pond. This is necessary, too,
for the Friday night game in a bandbox gym
on the Tennessee border, the crowd so shrill,

the teams keep playing long after the whistle.
In the last three minutes, every score
or close call sets off noise like a saw hitting metal.

It is all so simple, just then.
A single point down, only one breath left on the clock,
he slides by a pick at the top of the key,

and is out of himself,
is fingertips, wrist, elbow, and eyes.
When the shot clicks softly on the bottom of the net,

he can hear it.

HOMEWORK

I explored the old frame house half torn down
by whoever owns it now,
and a cloud like blueblack smoke rolled in,
the wind grew loud. I was alone
on someone else's land, yet I believed
history had written me a warrant
to walk where my grandmother lived sixty years;
where the family would gather every May
when the first honeysuckle was in bloom.
The wind blew hard. What I found,
a yellowed sheet wedged in a crack,
was algebra in Lilla Mae's hand, with the date
April 27, 1910.
She had solved for the 8 unknowns on the front
but had written on the back "Find the sum
of the flowing." Nothing followed.
And I tried to give an answer, tried to add
the heartpine boards to the rain-sweetened air,
the ash-fine dust to my grandmother's voice,
a whisper in the storm; tried to add
the old slow Sunday afternoons; then the wind,
as if helping, swept the paper from my hand.

THE SECRET

Our father always said, "Remember this:
however good you are, someone's better." Every March,
teased by an early warm day,
my brother and I, both backyard stars,
resumed our climb toward the majors.
Maybe Greenville for a while or Chattanooga.
Who had not spent time with a farm team? Still,
we expected Ebbets Field.

And our father's sad logic didn't hold. All it took
was the sports page pulled from *The Journal* —
Willie Mays in the league's top spot, or someone else.
But the spot itself was there, so why not us?

I think of all the days when he came home late,
the light nearly gone, walked straight to the yard
in his tie and good shoes, threw us batting practice,
hit us hard ground balls; and repeatedly,
because we were afraid, showed us how
to play the ball and not to let the ball play you;
to take it in the chest if you had to.

I can see him there, balanced on his toes,
in a low crouch, ready for the grounder —
how the tie that he had thrown across his shoulder
has slipped off now, falling nearly to the dirt,
his eyes still fixed on the ball coming fast,
as if that one chance were his last.

SOME WORDS FOR BILL MATTHEWS

Those cold eyes aimed our way made it clear
we had laughed too hard. You proposed
words for the look that she had given us:
mirth control, you called it.
                              And today,
when I thought of that quip once again,
remembering how *silly*, in an early sense, meant
blessed in the spirit, I had gone out
shopping for a used car.
                              Everywhere I went,
they were calling old heaps *pre-owned*,
as though a service had been done:
they had pre-worn brake pads down, pre-bent
the fender, pre-replaced the alternator,
they'd pre-rebuilt the clutch.
                              So each of us
is used; we're all vehicular: the word
takes us for a spin.
It honks the horn, violates the laws, gets us lost,
and trades us in.
                              The motor of the old new car
gave a low smoker's laugh
as I drove it off the lot this afternoon.
The jazzy bad news buzzed the radio. The road
moaned its only tune.

THE QUESTION

1.

It stank like ripe fish, milk gone bad —
that store on Polk Road owned by Jackie Neal,
who saw it as a nation set apart,
a country where he got to make the laws: King Jackie,

ruler of the aisles; highest court
over every word spoken, over mops fallen still;
the keeper of the key to the toilet, absolute
owner of the tips. When he kicked me

with his steel-toed boots one morning, he explained
he didn't need a reason. He would spew
philosophies of race all day:
they looked like apes; holy scripture had decreed

their servitude forever; all they wanted
was to lie around in bed eating pigs' feet;
they bred like dogs; if you put them in the jungle,
they'd be swinging on vines, talking gibberish,

and wearing no clothes, and it wouldn't take a week.
What's more, Jackie said, they'd be happy there,
where they came from. I should have set him straight,
so this would be a story with at least

a trace of heroism, but it's not. I had heard
words like Jackie's all my life. I believed
people wouldn't change, and other things
occupied me then: Carla Middlebrooks

and the ride we would take each night, cruising out
in her father's old rattletrap Ford,
getting lost on purpose, every back road new,
the weed fields sweet, moon floating on the lake,

crickets in the grass, tires rasping underneath.
Nothing else mattered, not the store's rotting air,
not Jackie's unremarkable soliloquies. The one
black man working at the store — he was called

Chickenbone; I never knew his real name —
had endured Jackie's talk for half his life,
at sixty years of age still a bag boy, a boy
with grandchildren. Chickenbone and I, that day,

leaned back lazily, our crossed feet propped
on the stock — he had bought us both candy,
put his money on the register because
no one had a key — and then he told me,

chuckling just a bit at the white boy, what
was obvious, he said, but I'd never even guessed:
Jackie sold sugar to the moonshiners.
There's a damaged half grin that can stay

on the face of a man knocked stupid.
It was something like that, only different, the way
we gazed across the cans at one another,
having both only heard it at the store. We were not

glad, yet not quite sad. Satisfied
might say it — how we felt, kicked back like that,
knowing they had hauled Jackie Neal's shackled body
from the bottom of a creek in Franklin County.

2.

In a well-known photograph, a black man's chained
to a bed frame. Assembled with the body
are the people who have lynched him. And it's clear
the photographer has tried to get the crowd in,

since the dead man's far to the left, relegated
to the scene's dim periphery, as if
he were almost irrelevant. Against
a boredom so thick it made me slow, I created

a perverse entertainment,
and now, nearly thirty years later,
it reminds me of the boys I have read about
who crawled for adventure near a fence

to sneak a look at Auschwitz:
I convinced two friends, and we drove out together
to a meeting being held in a cow pasture.
My parents had forbidden me to go,

shouted that I knew it wasn't right. Yes, I did,
but my argument was this: I'd rise above it;
I would study them with clinical detachment,
those idiots in sheets and pointed hats.

My parents didn't buy it, made me promise.
I promised them. I said the words and went.
When I look at that photograph now, it is not
the mutilated man I return to —

who appears strangely free — but the crowd
posing for eternity and squeezing in tight,
smiling for the camera. A head leans in
at the picture's edge, not to be denied

its rightful place. The gathering was this:
a long worship service, with the choir
in slightly different robes. I won't forget
the beauty of the cross. I often think

of standing there quietly; and how, out of habit,
when the leader of the group raised his hand
and commanded everyone to bow his head,   .
without a thought, at first, that's what I did.

3.
I'm watching television with my son — blacks and whites
holding yet another forum
on the question. I don't tell him, but I think,
as I hear what fills those voices, there are things,

ordinary things, that can never be redeemed.
Frances Sheats worked thirteen years for my mother,
made a dollar every day. I can see her
standing at the stove, cooking turnip greens,

feigning anger as she runs me from the kitchen;
Frances, who would have no children of her own;
whom I came across once crying hard in the pantry,
and who looked me in the eyes but wouldn't answer.

She is gone now; history has taken her from where
she never should have been — in our rocking chair,
the old hymns mellow in her throat,
her low hum lulling me to sleep. She is lost

from all I'm free to love. One afternoon,
at a movie matinee, painted Africans
throwing spears chased a hero with a gun
across a rope bridge strung above a river.

An older boy behind me started shouting
to the white man — cut away the ropes, he advised:
if the blacks tumbled in, they would die,
as everybody knew they couldn't swim. Back at home,

when I asked her to explain what I had heard,
Frances shook her head, then pulled me to her lap
and held me like she did when I was tired.
The panel on the show grows loud at the end.

My son and I discuss what they have said,
and he walks off slowly to his room,
moves heavily; and firing up his amp,
plays hard, wailing riffs he has inherited

from unnamed men with their second-hand guitars,
who are still there, sitting on the back steps, long
after dark, after coming home burdened with the fields,
the factories, the kitchens, or the streets — no words

equal to their histories of loss, or at least
nothing you will ever hear from me.

TWO LOVE LETTERS

From a Young Man

Dear Maria, Think of this:

A house beside the ocean, no one else
for miles; lazy mornings, long talks
over breakfast on the terrace, where the sea

is the color of an old tattoo;
where the cool salt breeze, faintly sweet, cuts the sun;
where the only star that matters to the skin

glistens in the oil on our bodies; where the waves
count slowly, and the clocks seem to follow,
till the days stall out, then dissolve;

where the gauzy white curtains hang open, so the sun
reflecting off the water washes in,
across the rumpled bed's cool sheets; and at dawn,

where the gulls' shrill calls fill the air, we'll belong
to the soft word *pillow*, how it flows
from touching lips, lifting with the tongue, whispers

oh.

From an Old Woman

> Dear Clarence, After supper last night,

I brewed me a cup of strong coffee, took it out
on the front porch and sat in that swing. (I imagine
you'll remember that swing.) It was hot,

and I opened my blouse to feel the breeze,
if one should ever rise. You will laugh, I know —
there I was, undressing in the heat

and drinking hot coffee at the same time. Remember
how we used to watch the lights across the valley.
We could follow one car as it curved along the ridge,

till it rose out of sight. And I recall
how you made up stories for the drivers, how
at times it wouldn't even be a story, just

a sentence or a phrase. *There's a man in that car
who can't hold a job.* And you whispered, once,
as though to yourself, *She's beautiful.* Clarence,

my life is not over. If you come here,
remember those pills for your heart. Last night,
I prepared scented water for my bath,

and I washed my body like a bride. Afterwards,
as I lay in the hot dark, touched by the breeze
at last, I imagined I was waiting for you,

and all at once, Clarence, I was.

THE FOOLISHNESS OF GOD
IS WISER THAN MEN

— 1 Corinthians 1:25

God's editors erased what they thought not right:
the lighter side of Christ, how Jesus laughed,
delighted, pierced with irony, surprised.

A child's first word could have done it;
or the feel of water firm beneath his feet;
or Pilate's simple question "What is truth?"

I believe he caught his sandal on a root;
that he shook his head, chuckling at himself,
humbled, but renewed; that it was men

who could not quite handle what it meant: Christ,
blessed by a great joke, going to his knees,
saying "mercy," saying "please."

ELEGY FOR A YOUNG POET

Better to be
The tree
Than the ants
Working on this blue day …
                    — from "Sunday" by Bill Richard, Jr.

You knew this, Bill: all elegy will fail,
every word turn to air; that we are all

like autumn leaves, unconscious in the sun.
They turn, shine, dazzle, whisper, fall.

You knew this too, how the days
and the seasons that can never come again

must come again. The trees,
the rest of us, have work that must be done.

And one long blue day glory comes down
like the light in old photographs, son.

A WORLD BENEATH

1.
We set about the task, dragged the mattock,
the post hole digger from the shed
and divined the right spot beneath the oak.
I swung the pick six or seven times,

and the tool pulled me downward in its wake.
Resting in the shade, I came to think
if we didn't work faster,
we wouldn't get to China until well past dark.

But I wondered who would pull us up again
from the country that was always underneath,
where the people might never have heard
they were living in a miracle —

a world beneath another;
how they dangled upsidedown but did not fall.

2.
Dropping to the ground, unlacing heavy high-tops,
peeling off grimy white socks,
I stepped onto cool cut grass
as the pines and the live oaks blackened, the brick

of the small house giving up the buttery glow
only sundown brought. It was time
to run alone over that chilled green shadow
where the yard sloped down toward the chickenwire,

and to ask, not calling up the syllables, but
in the language of blue jeans flapping at my ankles,
if anyone could run that fast.
And there came no answer, only this:

the chuckle of my father's Chevrolet, as it rolled,
slowly, down the long gravel driveway.

3.

On a bright late August afternoon, Uncle Johnny
lit a thin panetella, and the rich, bitter smell
mingled with the odor of manure, carried
on a hot breeze cutting through a hog farm

to linger in my grandmother's yard. They had laid
the long two-by-eights across saw horses
and loaded those makeshift tables
with roast beef, barbeque, skillet-fried chicken,

collard greens, field peas, tart pickled peaches,
gallon jars of iced tea sweeter than the pies.
And when the heat waves liquified the air
near the barn's tin roof,

the men lay beached on the screened front porch,
many with the same long nose, same chin,
but they all showed the heaviness; their eyes
tried to close.

4.

There is only one story of hunting I can tell.
At twelve, I would drift in the far back pasture
of my grandfather's dairy farm,
firing at pine stumps, limbs, tin cans

balanced on outcroppings. Often I would load
the single-shot .22, draw a tight bead
on a buzzard in a slow arc brushing the clouds,
try to gauge how far I should lead him,

then carefully squeeze. Never once
did I ruffle a feather,
so I turned back finally to things close by.
I could say I didn't really want to kill,

but to move one finger and to change
the heavens, yet in truth,
what I wanted was to watch a body fall that far,
and to hear it hit the earth.

5.

When the small white flowers of the blackberry flare
then quickly disappear,
the cool dusk air fills with honeysuckle,
and a smell still comes from the cotton fields:

like a crossbreeze washing through a cellar,
a faint ammonia cut with musty weed
that can sting the eyes bright. Driving home
on the blacktop Sunday afternoon,

when my daughter's face twisted with her question,
I inhaled the insecticide deeply, drew it in
till it touched every summer of my life; I explained
it was poison, though I drove on slowly, and as if

I could never get enough.

PRAYER

Who is equal to a seed, piece of wood, plain rock,
or any simple thing? Whose words are enough
for the ocher leaf floating to the earth

on the journey of its life? Who can rise
to its falling; who will feel it on his tongue,
the oak's new foliage of sky? So if we

should find no words in a graveyard, where's
the bulletin in this? Let us practice,
in unison, our lullaby of silence.

Let us offer each glance, every step
we take among the graves as a paying of respects,
but in ways we can't conceive. And if the past

should gather like a storm, loom ahead;
and if the future should return
as a room closed off now, windowless and still,

let us lift a bit of dust or blade of grass
and release it here, an offering to the air,
a brief, mute prayer for the breeze — easy lover

of the skin, lonely mother of the breath.

CALVIN'S WIFE

In Puritan belief, each shuffle of the cards,
or rolling of the dice was a sin.
But not because the players put their families at risk,
and not because gain came easily, or that
it happened most often in the alehouse, home
to Jezebels and drunks. What really mattered
was the window into providence. Because
the Lord set forth his plan in every breeze,
each petal as it fell, every filament of dust
twisting at the windowsill, *chance*
was a heathen word, offered by the lost.
So it followed: any showing of the deal,
all rolling of the soothsayer's bones
was a trifling with design, a sleazy glance
at holiness. But there she is again
in the line at the Quickie Mart, buying one shot
at the powerball. Tonight,
when she walks outside with her ticket,
a haze of bugs swirls above the gas pumps, wild
with the light — every feint, flit, and swerve
invisibly determined. If she wins,
she'll quit her job, her hair will never smell
like the poultry plant again. She will invest,
let the money do the work, let someone else
check the chicken guts for spots, and yet the God-
given odds tell us this:
tomorrow, she'll be up before the sun,
put the ugly green uniform on, pop the hood
of Calvin's old Ford to get it started, as she does
every day. Chances are,
when the dying car coughs itself to life,

and she rolls off slowly down the road,
where the wet streets gleam as if shined by hand,
where the windowpanes blaze blackened red,
where the paper trash scatters with the breeze,
she will let herself praise another day, made glad
as if God still numbered every hair
on her head.

GOING HOME

You have seen these women at the steering wheel,
an old man riding in the right front seat,
his heart unreliable, his eyes finding haze,

or maybe he is mapping out routes to a home
only in the past. All of us
have followed those old women going too slow

down two-lane roads. We have taken our place
in the long line of cars. And some of us,
released by a straightaway, raise one palm

in disbelief, the other hand steady on the horn.
We roar past, brandishing a face. Later on,
we'll come to understand she's not the problem,

which is always, somehow, time.
It's the sun too bright on the asphalt slick
with afternoon rain; it's the cloud brought low

in the field beside the road; the crackling hiss
of the tires racing past. And which of those
old women going home doesn't know this?

LAUGHTER

1.

If a line of cars following a hearse rolls past,
local custom still obtains: until it's gone,
every other car occupies the shoulder of the road.
But today, there's a hearse with a flat tire
by the highway, the undertaker's men working fast,
like a pit crew called out far too close
to the checkered flag. Lug nuts freeze,
so the funeral has stalled beside the road
and the protocol's reversed:
the ordinary traffic travels on; behind the hearse,
relatives and friends sit waiting to resume
the afternoon chore. They are not, all of them,
solemn in their grief — some laugh,
as if greatly entertained; we can see it. As for us,
perhaps we're amused now too, maybe we
are silly with a pain all our own, driving off
laughing as if cracked along the funnybone.

2.

After three days losing what he ate,
he was waiting at the hospital, hearing people talk
in the next small cubicle. A man said, "Well,
the cancer's in my liver now, they think."
A woman's voice broke, saying, "Honey."
The eavesdropper's stomach made a fist, so he stood,
pulled the IV rack to the toilet, where he sat
and answered them, not wanting to. As though
inspired, he played a note so raw, so pure,
the tears next door turned to poorly hidden laughter,
a rasping that was fast, then slow, then fast;
and mortified, feverish with shame, he couldn't help
feeling, at the same time, something
he didn't understand. It was as though
he'd known them all his life, and always loved them.

3.

The man next door makes the world news. First,
little girls all over town, including yours,
begin to disappear. The authorities will find,
much later, he has lured them to his house,
and what he's done then,
no one must imagine, since the news tells it all.
He cuts them up and puts them into food
he delivers each time (this does him in)
to the folks whose child he has violated. Say
you recall what the casserole tasted like,
the bites he made you eat against your appetite,
insisting he had gone to so much trouble;
how he said he'd made it special, just for you.
And when everyone's familiar with the news,
in breakrooms, schoolyards, offices, and bars,
the jokes will metastasize, laughter will arise.
This will happen not too far from where you are.

4.

The old man drove out Snow's Mill Road,
and he walked across the fields some real estate concern
had divided into lots. There was not one hint
of the small frame house, not a trace
of anything that moved — nothing there
of bird dog, wagon wheel, sweet white sheets
lifting in the breeze. The developers had cut
the old oaks, leveled off the hills, even made
the road go straight where it shouldn't have, so
the homeplace seemed like a lie he had told,
all his life, to himself. And then he chanced
on the concrete slab that capped the well,
and he stepped off the distance to the back porch,
entering the kitchen, turned to frame
the windows with his hands; he found the stove,
the icebox, the round oak table; slowly walked
through the whole gone house, as if morning had arrived,
time to wake the others. And he recognized the sky,
and he heard his own laughter, and he recognized the air,
and he stood there.

THE WIDOW'S DESIRE

1.
If some things happen for a reason, she believes,
others simply are.

As she looks on, sitting by herself
near the back one bleak Sunday morning;
as the gospel choir starts on the chorus

following a long, slow verse; as the man,
with one quick sweep of his arm, sets the choir
swaying to a picked-up rhythm —
                              this is what
gives her such a chill, this coincidence —

as the man whips the group into step,
as the bright new unison begins, just then,
the sun comes streaming through the windows,

as if the song brought a change in the weather
or the heavens had rehearsed with the choir.

2.
She finds herself following a baseball team
on the TV. Secretly, she talks
to the players and the manager.

                              She knows
the nicknames. Picking up the paper,
she checks on the average of the catcher,
in the slump of his career.

                              She develops
an opinion on artificial turf, as her boys
lose too often on the rug,
and it's ugly.

                    She understands the trouble
in the bullpen. Her own arms ache
when they talk about the cortisone shots
for the shortstop's elbow.

                    Now,
on a clear, perfect evening in June,
she can go to bed saddened by the rain.

3.
Mary Ann Laney's lost her job, and there she is,
raising those children alone.
Willie Connor's got cancer. Carl Sims

has some trouble with the law. All assembled
in the basement of the church hear the names,
and they pray for each one.
                    Then at home,
when she turns off the late world news,
those faces on the screen keep crying —
people she will never see again, whose grief

she has just clicked off.
The telephone rings. There is no one on the line.
Another ring. No one.
                    When it rings
again, she could slap God hard, the way she would
any man she loved
who remained where he was, watching anything at all,
without a word.

4.

Talking on the phone to her sister, she begins
looking at the moths on the windowpane,
the brown wavy marks on their papery wings
like layers of waterstain.

                          Static on the line
interrupts, and they talk about the static,
then the prices at the market downtown,
the bargains this week.

                          Hanging up,
she thinks about standing in a barn, long ago,
waiting out a thunderstorm; how,
when the rain slacked off, she and Charles
had kept on standing in the door.

                          Her desire
is to breathe that air once more,
cattle smells and wet pine rising on a breeze
sweetened by the rain,

                          to claim the air
washing in cool through a cornfield,
across the oily hot motor of the John Deere.

5.
She dreams there is someone in the house, dreams
she goes down into the basement,
clatters through the tools till she finds it,

and eases up the steps with a hammer. Halfway,
it grows too heavy for her arms.
But someone's in the house,

and the sound now comes from the basement.
She opens up a door off the stairwell, a door
she has never even seen. And underneath

her own small house, she discovers
another one — a large, warm home. Somehow,
a family has gathered, and a silly little boy

makes everybody laugh, and she stands there
quietly at the door,
wondering who they are.

THE MULTITUDE

The woman in the airplane wanted
to talk about Christ. I did not.
I raised my magazine. She continued, saying Christ
promised heaven to the thief
who believed while nailed to the cross.
The clouds looked solid far beneath. She began
the story of her life, and I stopped her
as politely as I could, saying please, right now,
I'd simply like to read. And for a while,
she did keep quiet, then she asked
if I'd ever really given Christ a chance, so I tried
telling her a joke, chose the one
about the Pope and Richard Nixon in a rowboat.
She discovered nothing funny in the story.
Jesus fed the multitude, she said.
I looked around to find an empty seat.
There wasn't one. She asked me if I knew
about the sower and the seed; about Zaccheus;
Legion and the swine; Mary Magdalene;
Lazarus; the rich young ruler. And I did,
I knew about them all. I told her yes,
sweet Jesus; got the stewardess
to bring another bourbon; tried to buy
the missionary one, but she declined.
And when the plane set down,
I'd escaped up the aisle, made the door,
and started walking fast toward the baggage claim,
when I saw them, all at once, on the concourse:
thousands I would never see again, who'd remain
nothing in my life, who would never have names;
and I realized I'd entertained — strangely,

and for no good reason I could see —
the hope of someone waiting there
who loved me.

SUSTENANCE

We talk about food over the phone.
My mother wants to know if I have eaten,
and I think about the funny old photographs
of babies barely wedged into highchairs, spoons
raised to our round, fat faces
as long as we would swallow,
and we'd swallow until sleep drooped us over.
We talk about white corn, canteloupe, tomatoes.

In the first year living by herself,
my mother looked starved,
like a refugee in clothes not her own.

This evening, while the soup was on the stove,
I called her, and I told her what was in it:
a sweet Vidalia onion, new potatoes; I detailed
the way I planned to eat it later on —
with the cornbread ready for the oven, mixed
exactly as she taught me. We discussed
the touch of oil added to the cornmeal — how
some varieties are better for the heart —
and then grew quiet. There are times,

like tonight, when the silence we allow
on the telephone holds for us both, I believe,
such a difficult ease, it is almost grace.

HOME

The stroke-addled old folks drooling all day;
the women holding baby dolls, calling them by name;
the swollen-tongued toothless in their wheelchairs;

the wrinkled infants sitting in their own fresh waste;
the mange-haired talkers with their questions;
the skeletons with clothes on, skulls wearing skin

like tissue paper pasted on the bone — on and on,
the wailing wall-eyed horror that they were
when I first appeared among them with my mother.

Then a history of groans began to grow,
till the sing-song noise made sense; till the wild
rocking side to side said welcome; till the mouth

locked forever in its *O* spoke of home.

SURRENDER

We were ordinary men,
unable to embrace each other fully —
to bury a face in the other man's neck,
to rock like drunks in the doorway, saying
goodbye. It was always a handshake
and maybe that sideways hug,
with an arm around the shoulders.

                               In the hospital
you couldn't understand, didn't know me,
tried to overturn the rack by the bed, tear
the needles from your arm; searched everywhere,
underneath the sheets and the pillow,
for your clothes, *going home;* grew frightened
when confused by the purpose of a spoon, angry
when you couldn't even urinate — failing
to hit the plastic bottle, till I held you.
If I leaned down close
when the baffled agitation started up,
and I smoothed back your hair, or I kissed you
on the forehead or the cheek, whispered "Daddy,"
you'd throw your arms around me.

There's a way a man turns to a woman,
so his lips just barely graze hers, yet in this,
there is everything that follows, each detail
of forgetting where they are.
And today I am trembling with desire, wild
for the years, when my lips feel yours, cool
as gold. One kiss for the infinite
particulars of love, to tell you this:

I will be with you there, in the darkness.

DESIRE

I cut my mother's nails. If a nursing home aide
should offer to, they tell me, she declines,
explaining that her son will do it soon.
                                    And when I'm done,
she studies how they feel, and if she finds
any roughness, lets me smooth it with a file.
I'm careful with the quick beneath her nails; the ten o'clock
angle that her right thumb forms at the knuckle;
arthritis that can freeze either wrist. Last week,
she told me she was thirsty while I worked.
I poured a glass of water, helped her hold it as she drank.

She looked at me and said, "Such pretty eyes.
Did anybody else ever tell you that?"
She offered me the glass and then her hand.

I remember Daddy telling us the story
of the days before they shipped him out to war;
how Mama took the train to California.
From the window of their room they saw the desert,
and perhaps for the last time waking up together,
they saw the mountains burn, they saw the blue
spilling through the valleys.
                                    Daddy never told the rest,
but then they must have turned to one another;
for all their stolen dawns, they must have gathered up the sky,
the mountains, the tomorrows, and the war, in their desire.

This morning when I start to leave her room,
she calls my name but can't remember why.

                             And then I'm gone,
but not before I've kissed her once again,
and not before we've smiled and almost told
each other what we want.
                   It is the world.

A POSTCARD TO MY FATHER

Alone in a strange place now,
I often think of you,

and when the meeting broke early here in Jacksonville,
I walked back alone to my room,
made a drink, then relaxed on the balcony, the sea
indigo and palm-leaf green,
whitecaps far beyond the waves.

I lay across the bed, and then the dark
surprised me. I hadn't meant to sleep.

At dinner, people talked about the storm.
They had gathered at the windows of the bar
for the arteries of light branching out,
for the rain boiling silver on the asphalt,
for the palms bending low. You should have seen it,

they told me more than once,
you should have seen it.

IN THE SWEET BY AND BY

I had seen the earth open and close, the golden ash
of pollen wash away, each thin copper spine
of broomsage bending in the dawn,

as if burdened by the shining of the sun;
I had stared at the dirt; tried to reason what it meant
if the moon flared white on a wet tin roof,

if the clover bowed waving in the wake of every car,
if the petals of the dogwoods fell;
I had sat drinking coffee in the all-night diner,

with one good question for the universe
if people still joked at the counter,
if the hot grill hissed like rain,

if the rain fell softly in the parking lot;
like a slow child puzzled by a story's end,
I had kicked up dust to watch it float;

I had stumbled out stunned some days, like a boy
still lost in the afternoon movie, unprepared
for the late sun burning in the street;

but when I stood with my mother in the church,
a month since we had left him in the earth;
when the years swirled back like weather, there,

where the windows thrown open in July, long ago,
brought creosote and pine smells, freshly cut grass,
let the trucks' low groans on the highway rise

with every old anthem, every prayer;
where revivals once built all week like desire,
so the quiet in the worship hall crackled,

bristling with a charge, as if fire might arc
between the Word and the not-yet-saved;
where the preacher lay an everlasting weight

on the one final stanza we would sing;
where he pleaded with the lost until the yawn
of eternity began with the hymn's last note;

where I stood with my mother in the back row now,
found the melody and followed it, as though
there were nothing else to do; and when I heard

the alto my mother used to sing
at the ironing board or working in her flower bed
or standing at the sink, each note told the truth:

though the days break new in a mockingbird's throat,
and a gauzy mist stalls above a creekbed, spins,
as if conscious of its body in the light;

though a dying man can't help laughing at a joke,
so he rocks in his own wasted arms;
and a raincloud leans like a barn set to fall,

while the wind starts to whistle in the wires;
and though a woman lies back on the loading dock,
waiting for her ride while the sky turns red,

and a girl leaving work at the truckstop walks
toward a greasy strip of grass beyond the parking lot,
as the breeze cuts across the wisteria, its smell

mingled with the diesel and the smoke;
though the boys looking hard for a lost ball pause
for the brief wild sugar of the honeysuckle,

and a galaxy will whirl through the wilderness
like an oak leaf wheeling toward a roof; even though
the clover and the dogwoods bloom, we become

nothing, not the actors in a dream, not the mist,
not a new stone lowered into earth. We are like
the hymns once played on the out-of-tune piano

in the living room, harmonies defined
by the family that stood there — versions no one else
will ever reproduce. Sunday morning,

as we struggled through the chorus, there it was,
still, in my mother's soft alto — the old
promise in her voice.

AN INTRODUCTION

You who break the dark all night, whisper and shout,
who travel in and out of all the rooms,
who come with pill or needle, vial or chart,
with bedding, mop and bucket, tray of food;
who turn, clean, pull, read, record, pat, and go;
who see her hair matted by the pillow, greasy white
wild short hair that will shock
anyone from home who hasn't seen her for a while —
shocking like her bones, showing now;
like the plum-colored bruises on her arms; like her face
when she first comes to and what it says; like her mouth
and the anything it says: *Call the dogs,* or
I've got to go to school, or *Tonight y'all roll*
that wagon wheel all the way to Mexico; you
who have seen three children — unbelieving, unresigned —
in all these rooms, full of anger and of prayer;
you who change her diaper, empty pans
of green and gold bile she has puked up; you
who cannot help breathing her decay,

I would like to introduce you to our mother,
who was beautiful, her eyes like nightshade,
her wavy brown hair with a trace of gold; Myrtle,
whose alto flowed through the smooth
baritone our father used to sing;
our mother, who would make us cut a switch,
but who rocked us and who held us and who kissed us;
Myrtle, wizard typist, sharp with figures,
masterful with roses and with roast beef;
who worked for the New Deal Seed Loan Program,
for the school, local paper, county agent, and the church;

who cared long years for her own failing mother
(whom she worries for now; you may have heard her);
who was tender to a fault, maybe gullible,
as the truly good and trusting often are; and even so,
who could move beyond fools, though foolishness itself
delighted her — a double-take, words turned around,
a silly dance — and when our mother laughed
(I tell you this because you haven't heard it),
the world could change, as though the sun could shine
inside our very bones.
                              And where it's written in Isaiah
that the brier won't rise, but the myrtle tree,
there's a promise unfulfilled:
she will not go out with joy.
Still, if you had known her, you yourselves,
like Isaiah's hills, would sing. You'd understand
why it says that *all the trees*
of the field shall clap their hands.

ABOUT THE AUTHOR

Judson Mitcham's first collection of poems, *Somewhere in Ecclesiastes,* won the Devins Award and was published in 1991 by the University of Missouri Press. His work has appeared in many literary journals, including *The Georgia Review, Poetry,* and *Harper's.* His novel, *The Sweet Everlasting,* was published in 1996 by the University of Georgia Press. It won the Townsend Prize and was a finalist for the Southern Book Critics Award. Mitcham is an associate professor of psychology in the Department of Behavioral Sciences at Fort Valley State University. He has also taught creative writing at the University of Georgia, Emory University, and Mercer University. He lives in Macon, Georgia, with his wife, Jean, and they have two children, Zach and Anna.

WHAT, PRAY TELL, IS AN ANHINGA?

Closely related to cormorants, anhingas are found in the Deep South — most commonly in Florida. Our logo depicts an anhinga striking its signature pose, a stance the bird must hold for long stretches of time after each underwater fishing expedition because, lacking oil glands to dry them more quickly, its wings are too soggy to fly. The sinuous anhinga is also known as the snakebird for the way it swims with all but head and neck submerged below the surface of the water.

This April day :
811.54 MITCH   31057001378879

Mitcham, Judson.
WEST GA REGIONAL LIBRARY SYS   6/2003